MW01040036

Level 4

Masterwork Classics

Compiled and Edited by Jane Magrath

CONTENTS

May be
used with
*Alfred's Basic
Piano Library,*
as early as
Lesson Book 4.

Start *Masterwork
Classics* 4
after
page 25 in
Lesson Book 4.

Second Edition
Copyright © MCMXCVII by Alfred Publishing Co., Inc.
All rights reserved. Printed in USA.

Cover art: Planet Art

FOREWORD

Compositions in *Masterwork Classics* are among the best literature available at this level by the standard composers. All four periods of keyboard music are represented. The music was chosen because of its quality and accessibility. These works may be taught in a sequence that allows concepts learned in earlier sections in the volume to build upon one another.

Masterwork Classics 4 may be used as early as Level 4 of Alfred's Basic Piano Library. Students can begin to study these original classics by master composers after completing Lesson Book 4, page 25. These books are not correlated to Alfred's Basic Piano Library; they are designed to be used over a longer period of time than each Lesson Book. This volume and the others in this series can be used independently from the method.

Literature found in the *Masterwork Classics* series is drawn from the vast library of standard literature in high-quality editions issued by Alfred Publishing Company. As always, the highest editorial practices have been maintained in the compilation and editing of these works. Texts for the pieces are based on autographs or early editions. Editorial additions have been kept to a minimum. These few suggestions assist the teacher and student in rendering a stylistic performance of the work. For the literature from the baroque and classic periods, occasional fingerings, limited details of articulation, and sparse dynamic markings have been added by the editor. Suggested realizations of ornaments are provided in the margins. Literature from the romantic and contemporary periods contains sparsely added fingering when necessary and an occasional dynamic indication. Otherwise, the text is that of the composer.

Heartfelt appreciation is extended to Morton Manus, Willard Palmer, Maurice Hinson, and George Lucktenberg for their high editorial principles, for their scholarship, and for allowing the creation of this volume.

PRACTICE AND PERFORMANCE 4 —Student Practice Guide
to accompany
Masterwork Classics 4

Practice and Performance 4 by Jane Magrath contains practice guides for each piece in *Masterwork Classics 4*. It is written to the student for use by him/her when practicing. The material in the guide can be used by the student alone or with help from the teacher. The guide gives practice techniques for each piece of music in the following three stages:

GETTING READY TO PLAY—preparation

PRACTICE FOR PERFORMANCE—playing

FINISHING THE PERFORMANCE—evaluating what was heard and reworking the performance.

A major thrust of the volume is the development of the student's listening skills for performance. "Notes to the teacher" accompany the practice guide for each piece. Teachers will also be interested in the "Teacher's Thumbnail Guides" to performance considerations for each piece in *Masterwork Classics 4*. When lesson time is limited, *Practice and Performance 4* can aid the teacher by effectively organizing student practice techniques.

This order of study is suggested to allow playing requirements for each piece to build upon skills developed in earlier repertoire in *Masterwork Classics 4.*

Literature is listed in two columns since most students will study at least two pieces from this book simultaneously. This dual list allows contrast of style and sound for the student.

Voluntary

J.C. Pepusch
(1667-1752)

Andante maestoso

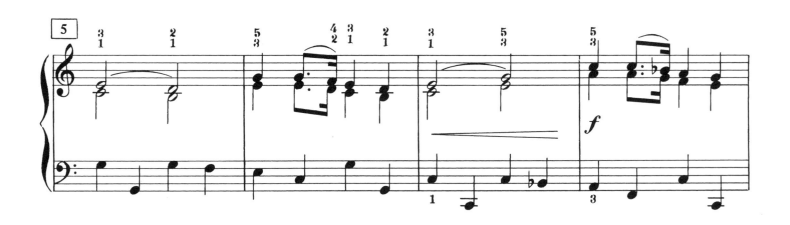

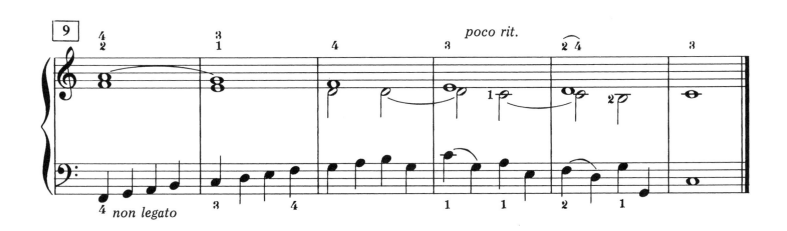

King William's March

Jeremiah Clarke
(1673-1707)

Maestoso

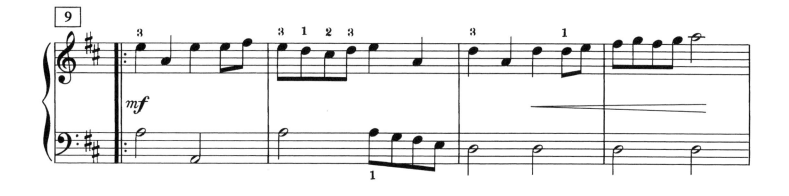

Menuet in D Minor

George Frideric Handel
(1685-1759)

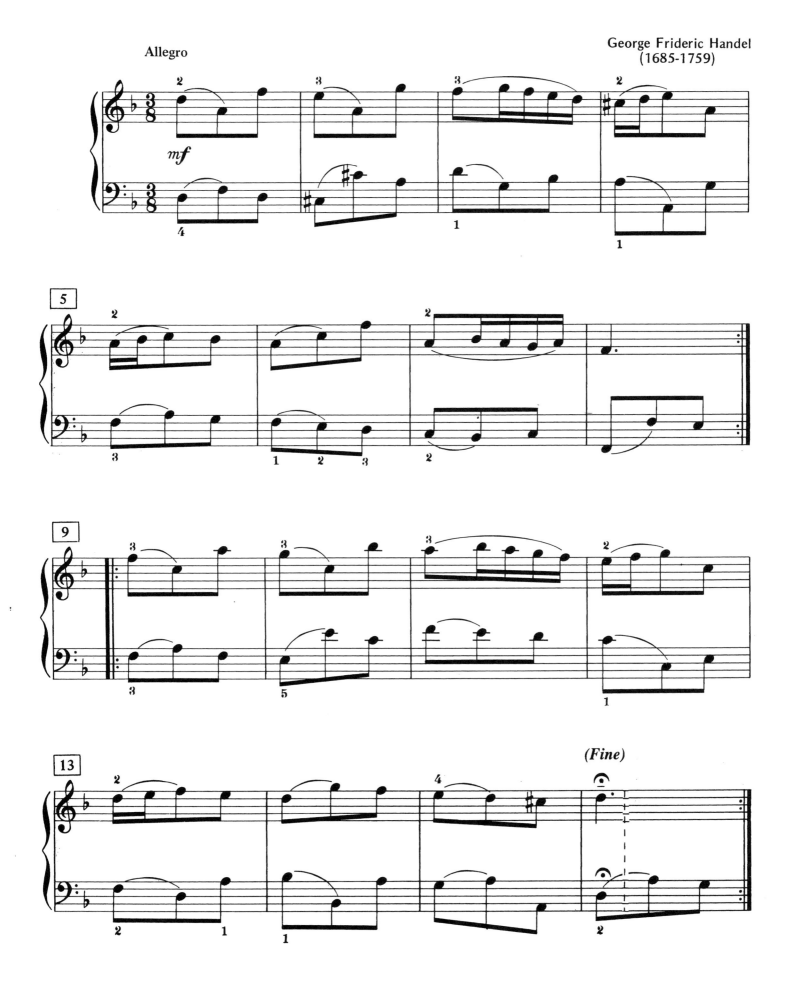

Air

Henry Purcell
(1659-1695)

Hornpipe

Henry Purcell
(1659-1695)

ⓐ These ornaments may be simplifed as shown: measure 4:   measure 8:   measure 12:

Menuet

(from Suite for a Musical Clock)

George Frideric Handel
(1685-1759)

Moderato

Menuet in G Major

BWV Anh. 116

from the *Notebook for*
Anna Magdalena Bach
(1725)

Un poco animato

ⓐ Most modern editions have D♯ here. The sharp does not appear in the original manuscript.

Menuet in G Minor

BWV Anh. 115

from the *Notebook for Anna Magdalena Bach* (1725)

Allegro moderato

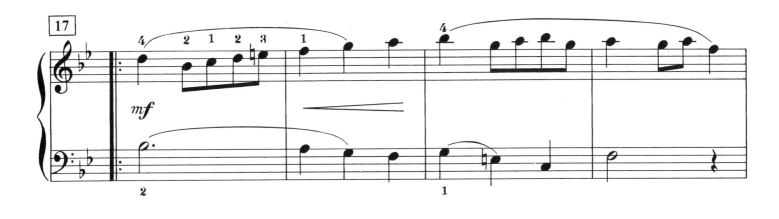

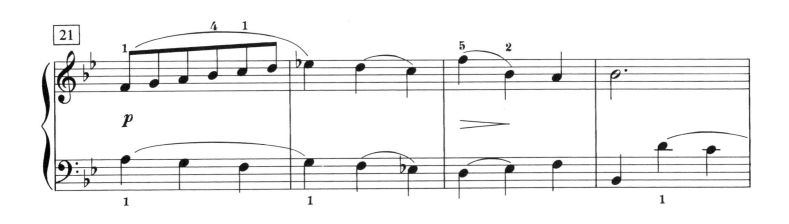

Polonaise in G Minor

BWV Anh. 119

from the *Notebook for*
Anna Magdalena Bach
(1725)

ⓐ The dotted rhythm may be exaggerated here and in the 5th measure.

Menuet in C Major

K. 6

W.A. Mozart
(1756-1791)

Allegro moderato

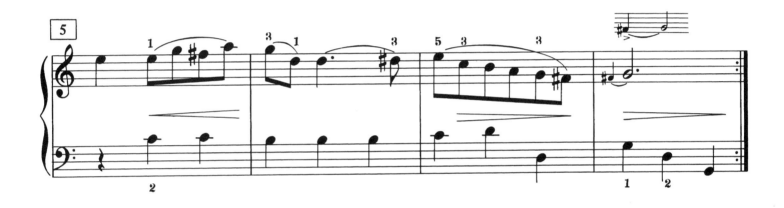

Pyrenese Melody

from Muzio Clementi's *An Introduction to the Art of Playing on the Pianoforte* (1801)

Allegretto

Country Dance in G Major

K. 15e

W. A. Mozart
(1756-1791)

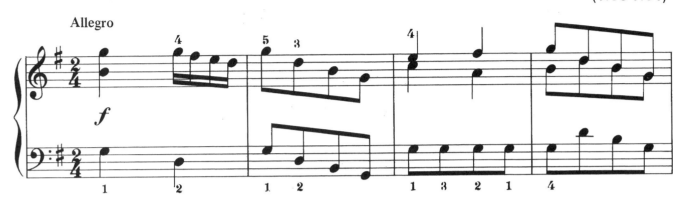

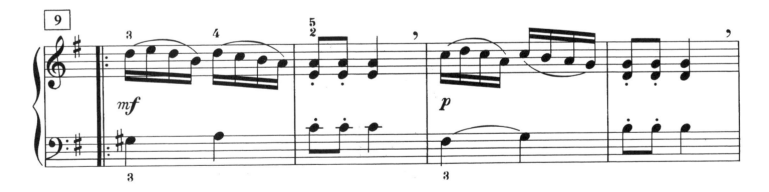

Sonatina in C Major

Tobias Haslinger
(1787-1842)

a tempo

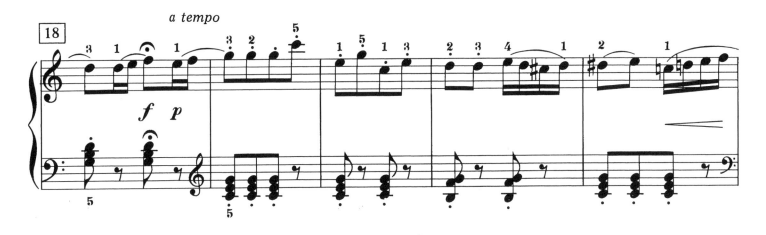

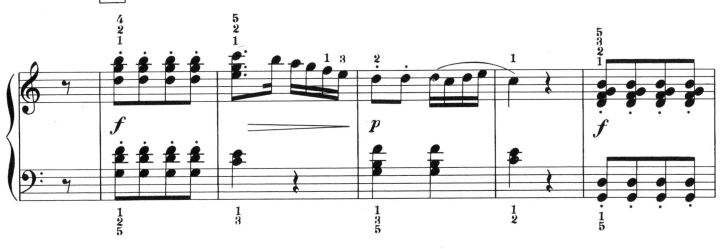

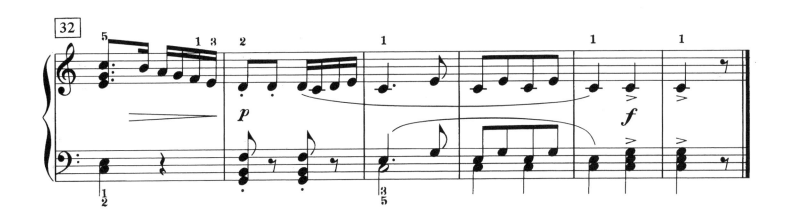

Scherzo in F Major

Hob. XVI:9

Franz Josef Haydn
(1732-1809)

Schwäbisch

(Swäbian Dance)

J.C.F. Bach
(1732-1795)

(a) At this period the wedge-shaped staccato marks indicate only that the notes are to be released instantly.

German Dance in C Major

WoO 13, No. 10

Ludwig van Beethoven
(1770-1827)

Country Dance in C Major

WoO 14, No. 1

Ludwig van Beethoven
(1770-1827)

German Dance in G Major

WoO 42, No. 6

Ludwig van Beethoven
(1770-1827)

Fine

TRIO

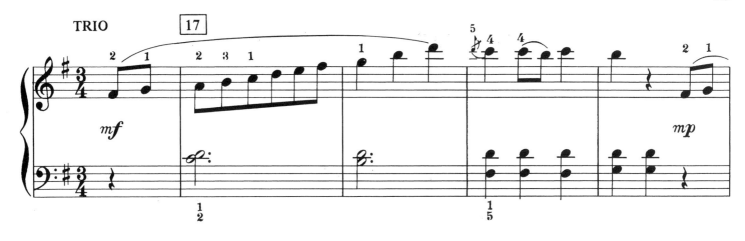

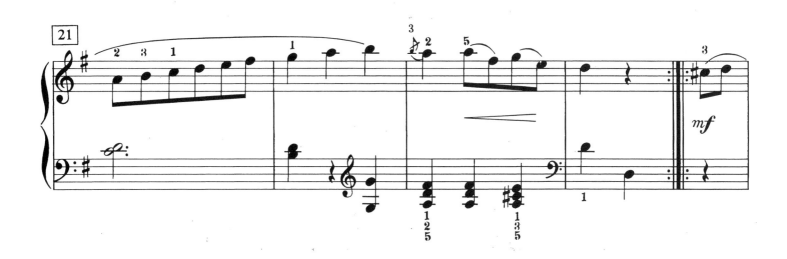

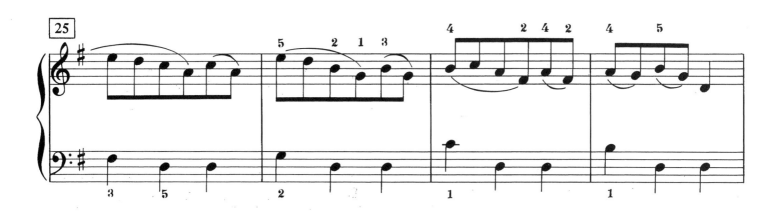

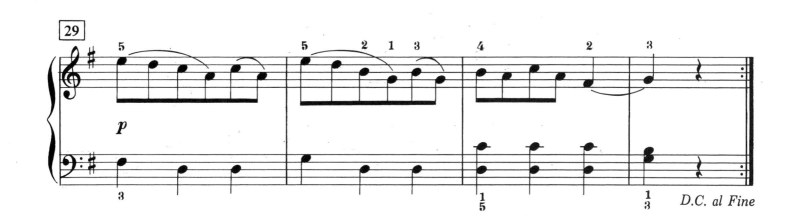

D.C. al Fine

A Pleasant Morning

Op. 63, No. 1

J.L. Streabbog
(J.L. Gobbaerts)
(1835-1886)

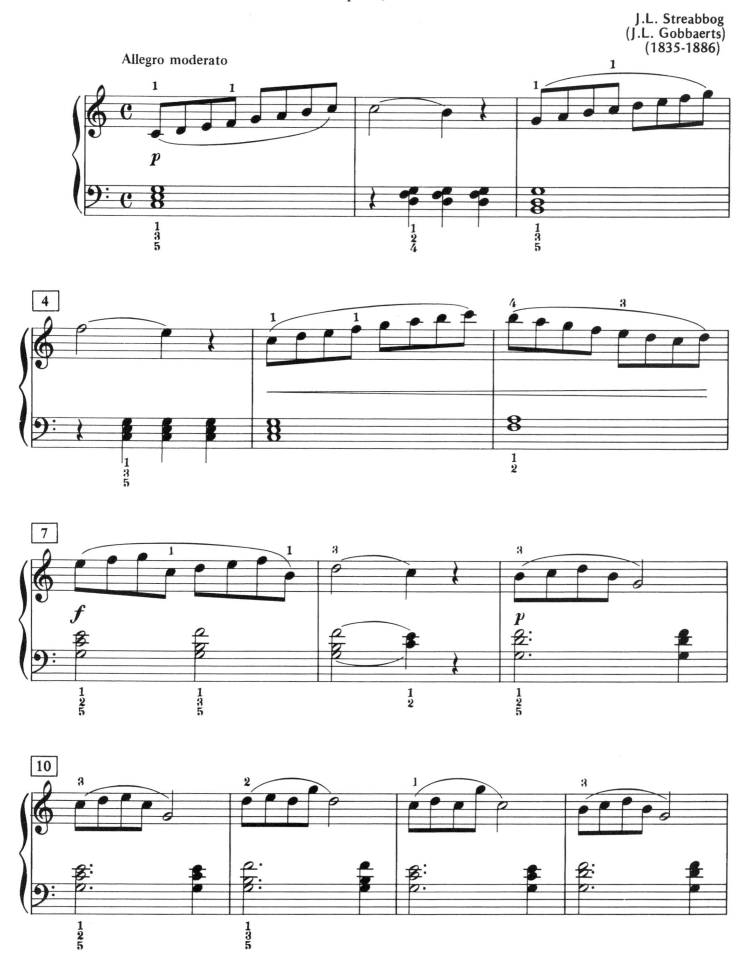

In the Garden

Op. 140, No. 4

Cornelius Gurlitt
(1820-1901)

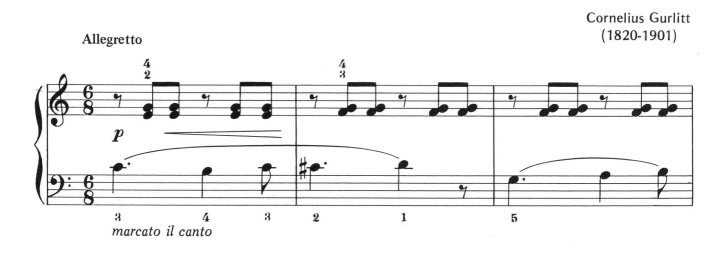

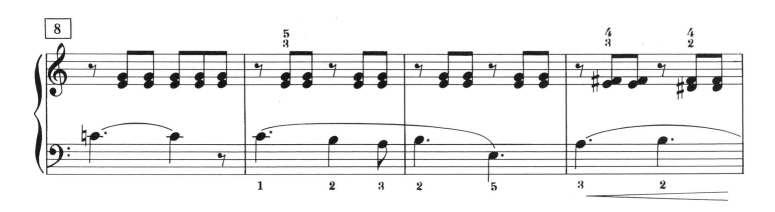

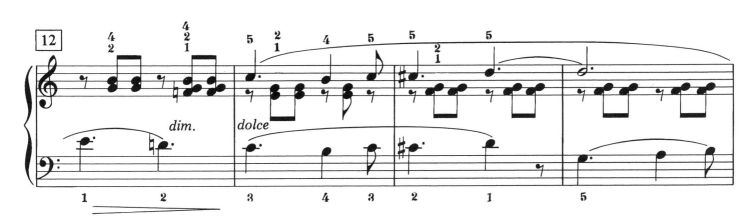

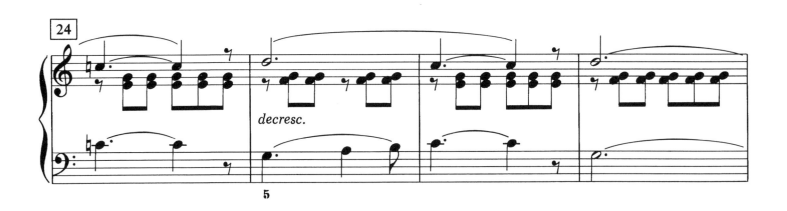

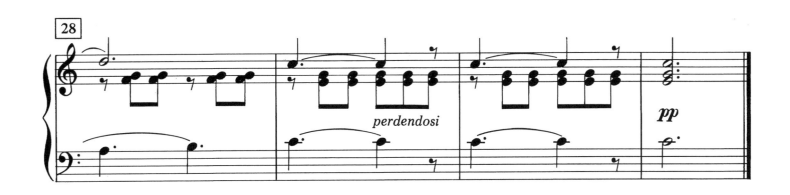

Murmuring Brook

Op. 140, No. 5

Cornelius Gurlitt
(1820-1901)

By the Seaside

Op. 63, No. 7

J.L. Streabbog
(J.L. Gobbaerts)
(1835-1886)

Serenade

Op. 140, No. 18

Cornelius Gurlitt
(1820-1901)

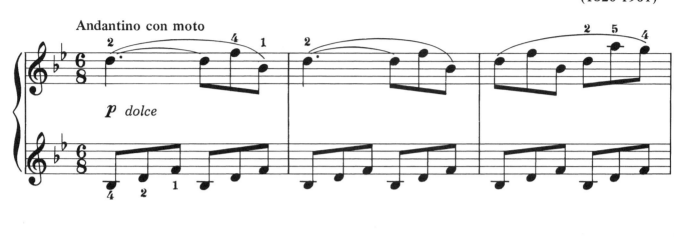

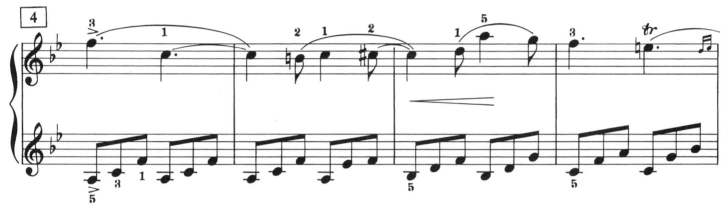

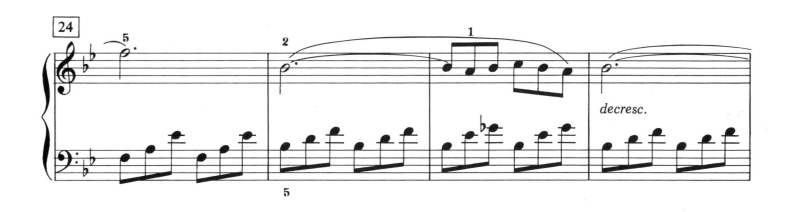

Arabesque
Op. 100, No. 2

Johann Burgmüller
(1806-1874)

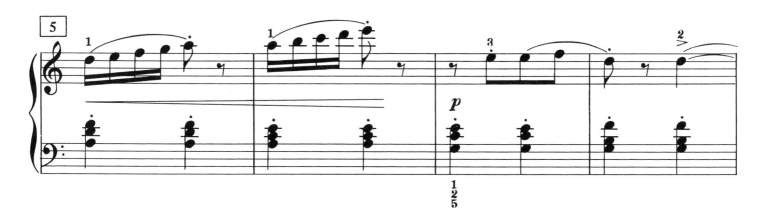

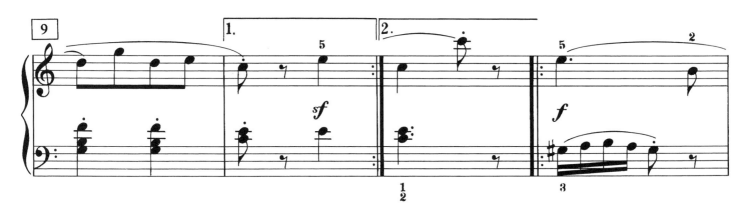

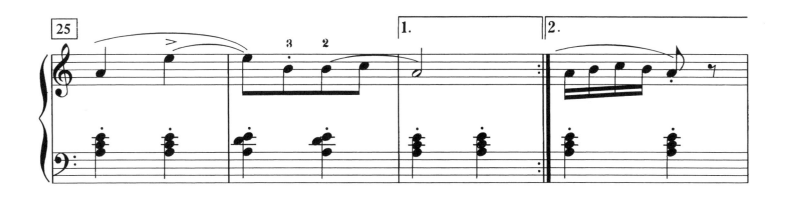

Progress
Op. 100, No. 6

Johann Burgmüller
(1806-1874)

Piano Piece No. VII

(from First Term at the Piano)

Béla Bartók
(1881-1945)

Piano Piece No. VIII

(from First Term at the Piano)

Béla Bartók
(1881-1945)

A Magic Game

Béla Bartók
(1881-1945)

Playing Soldiers
Op. 31, No. 4

Vladimir Rebikov
(1866-1920)

Galop

Op. 39, No. 18

Dmitri Kabalevsky
(1904-1987)

Clowns

Op. 39, No. 20

Dmitri Kabalevsky
(1904-1987)

Rhythmic Dance

Béla Bartók
(1881-1945)

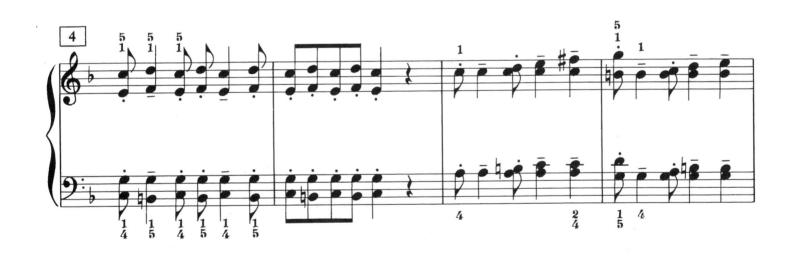

Hurdy-Gurdy

Dmitri Shostakovich
(1906-1975)

Etude

Op. 98, No. 12

Allegro

Alexander Gretchaninoff
(1864-1956)